A
Sassy Little Guide
to
Getting Over Him

A
Sassy Little Guide
to
Getting Over Him

10 Steps to Heal Your Heart After an Unhappy Ending

Sandra Ann Miller

SAME Ink

Author's Note: "I am not trained or licensed in the mental health fields and this book is not intended to nor should it replace counselling or therapy provided by a licensed professional. This book merely contains my philosophy on getting a breakup into perspective, based on and developed from my own experiences."

Published by SAME Ink
2554 Lincoln Blvd., #239
Venice, CA 90291 USA
Distributed by Lightning Source, Inc. US and UK
www.LightningSource.com

ISBN 1-4243-1525-5; 978-1-4243-1525-3

Printed in the United States of America

Angels can fly because they take themselves lightly.

— GK Chesterton

CONTENTS

Acknowledgements

Where would I be without the love and support of my friends? I would hate even to venture a guess. To go from first draft to print in eight weeks, it took a village of wonderful people championing this project on. And I am still in awe from the gifts I've received.

My deepest gratitude goes to each of my girlfriends who rallied with endless support and brilliant insight in the writing and publishing of this mini-tome. To Melissa Joy, Jordana, Dana J., Liz T., Kim B., Ellen V., Miwa, Caroline, Debbie W., Michelle M., Lisa, Summer, Sue B., Arianna, Sarane, Mary Louise and Patti for jumping into action with such zeal, my appreciation is endless. I am one lucky girl to have you in my life. I adore each of you so. To Cheryl T., Ellen F., and Sherrie S., for their generosity and gracious encouragement, a million thanks is merely the start, ladies!

To the men...all the men...who have brought me both joy and pain, *salute*. I have learned from every relationship. Some of the lessons were brutal, others were beautiful. I don't regret one of you... much.

To the men I regret not...Lawrence, with whom I have had the longest and healthiest relationship, I love you. As we near twenty years, I am pleased to know that I will grow older, and more fabulous, with you. James M., you have been such a wonderful friend and helped make this dream come true beyond my expectations. Thanks and love to you. Mike H., my treasured friend and mentor, besides love and thanks, I have one word for you: Mandarette! Mr. D., your support and good wishes have meant the world. You will always be my favorite father-in-law, even though we never got to make it official.

To Justin, my Jake, my favorite person on the planet...you taught me true love from the moment you were placed in my arms. I couldn't love you more if you were mine. And, as you become a man, I know you will be exemplary to every woman you love and to those who will love you.

To Starbucks store #5713 for the incredible Venti Soy Lattes, both iced and hot, that kept me fueled. You are the best. Thanks, friends!

Finally, last but certainly not least, to my dear friend Michiko...I will forever be indebted to your generosity with this project. Your talent, friendship, laughter and inspiration are gifts I cannot measure. You are absolutely fantabulous, girlfriend! It seems "W" was good for something after all! Thank you. Thank you! THANK YOU!!!

This book is dedicated to every girl
who's ever had a broken heart...
and lived to laugh about it.

To JLK,
whose breakup inspired the writing of this book.

And to Darren.
You were taken away much too soon.
You are one man I will never get over.

Introduction...

Dear Girlfriend,

One thing I'm confident we can agree on is that breakups suck. They are the emotional equivalent of a Brazilian wax. They transcend agony — going in to something so rotten we don't even have a word for it in the English language.

You feel like the wind has been kicked out of you, like your skin is being pulled off slowly...really, really slowly. The world as you've known it has come to a sorrowful, pitiful end. You are the definition of devastated. What's worse is that everyone seems to have a piece of advice to lend on the subject of breakups. Some say that the best revenge is looking good. Others say that the quickest way to get over a man is to get under another one. I don't believe either to be true; those theories make it all about *him*. This book is all about **you**.

I understand how bad it hurts because I've been there. Many times. I have gone through every kind of breakup there is: The Good, The Bad and The Utterly Excruciating. Having played both leading roles in my own breakup dramas and supporting bits in those of my friends, I've acquired certain breakup survival skills that I would like to share with you. It doesn't have to be a tortured experience. Really. You'll see.

While it might seem the natural thing to do, wallowing in the anguish of a breakup makes no sense. I mean, if you broke a leg, would you call all of your friends and tell them that you have a broken leg, cry about it, whine about the unbearable pain then hobble into bed, lie under the covers and wait for it to stop hurting? No. Not only is that irresponsible, it's just plain silly. If you broke your leg, you would call an ambulance, go to the emergency room, have the leg set, go home, get some rest, go to work, maybe even to a few parties, and have people sign the cast. You would get on with life and function as best you could while it heals.

Here's the smart broken-heart equivalent:

Call your best friend (the ambulance); go to your sofa, her house or a bar (emergency room options); have a good, hard cry (set the break); go home, get some rest, then go to work and maybe even a few parties; let people know what happened and allow them to buy you a drink (signing the cast); explain that you are on the mend and want to get on with life (function as best you can while you heal).

You are hurting now but you don't have to. You can get over him in ten simple steps. Yes. You can. That is, if you want to. If you do, read on. If you don't, put down the book and check yourself into a psychiatric ward directly. I mean, isn't it nuts to want to feel this bad?

Good. I'm glad you're reading on. You made the right decision. Now, take a deep breath and turn the page. You are one step closer to getting over him. *Congratulations!*

Cheers,

Sandra

The Ground Rules

Before we go any further, you need to make some promises to yourself. Raise your hand and repeat after me...

I, (state your name), do, hereby, solemnly swear that I will not behave in the manner of a crazy ex-girlfriend. I will not participate in foolish or destructive behavior. I promise to act in a dignified fashion and that means I will not do stupid things, no matter how I might rationalize them. Therefore, I vow the following:

1. I will not call him. No matter what good or bad news I think he should hear only from me, I will not call him. Even if I am convinced it will make me feel better, I will not call him. I will not call him even to get my stuff. I'll have a friend do that, preferably via email.

2. I will not email him. Not even an innocent

and rather funny group email forward. I will not email him simply to give him back his stuff. I will not contact him at all.

3.   I will not frequent the places I know he goes to, even if I went there first and like it better. I acknowledge that this is not a pissing contest about territory. I know going to such places will hurt more than it will help. Until there has been some space and time between us, going to those places is asinine, can be viewed as stalker-ish and will be painful only to me.

4.   I will not encourage or allow friends to do anything foolhardy, even with my best interest at heart. That includes talking to him when they see him in public to let him know he is a jerk and he'll never do better than me, or to share that I am looking fabulous, got a promotion, bought a new house and am dating George Clooney (or

the regional equivalent thereof).

5.   I will screen all of my calls. I will get Caller ID, if necessary, and put "private call block" on my phone. I will not answer the phone unless I know who it is and am sure it's not him. All other calls will go to voicemail.

6.   I will not take his phone calls. I repeat, I will not take his calls.

7.   I will not return his phone calls or emails. If he is "just checking" to see how I am, I know he is really just checking to see if I think he's a jackass. He is looking for an ego stroke, not to get back together, and I know this because he did not start out the communication with, "I am sorry. I made a mistake. I want us to get back together."

8.   I will not look for signs that we will get back together. This includes asking the

Magic 8 Ball or tarot card readers and the like. The only professional guidance I will seek will be that of a licensed therapist or member of the clergy.

9. I will not believe this is temporary. I will see this as permanent until proven otherwise by concrete actions, immense apologies and couple's therapy.

10. I will not hide under a rock, be humiliated or ashamed that this relationship ended. For all I know, this could be the best thing that ever happened to me. And I believe the wonderful stuff I deserve is on its way.

I promise to abide by these vows for at least thirty (30) days, or until I have gotten over him, whichever is longer. This is about me feeling better and that has nothing to do with him.

This I do affirm. So help me Me.

Signed: _____

Date: _____

Now you are ready to proceed. As you read on, remember the promise you have made to yourself. Enlist your friends in supporting this endeavor and keep in mind that this process is all about you and getting over him.

Step 1
Get Out of His Head

The first place women tend to go after a breakup is his head. You might be curled up in bed or a crumpled heap at your best friend's apartment, but you are living in his head. You've packed a bag, brought some groceries and have taken up residence, prepared to stay for as long as it takes to figure out what the bloody hell he was thinking.

There, in that dark, dank, dusty place, you relive every minute of the relationship and go over every word he said. You need to know two things: *Why* and *How*.

Why did it end?

How could he do or say all that he did and said if he didn't mean them?

Why can't we get back together and give it one more chance?

How can I live without him?

You go over his gray matter inch by inch, ridge by ridge, moving aside the piles of porn looking for a clue. Any clue. Somewhere there has to be a clue. You would give your right arm for a stinking clue! And when you can't find one that satisfies, you do what women tend to do...you resort to amateur psychology.

Most of us have taken a Psych class in college or have watched enough talk shows and made-for-TV dramas to be somewhat of an expert in human behavior. One season of *Oprah*® is really all you need, right? So, you go in and dig deeper. You reach all the way back to his childhood — or at least his last breakup — searching for more evidence as to why this went wrong. Now, every conversation you have with your friends, your family, your pet or (more sadly) yourself is a rumination on what past trauma(s) stunted him so that he was unable to handle you, your relationship or the realness of your love.

You spend days that turn to weeks, which turn to months, living in his head. At a certain point (and you aren't sure when), you were only able to form a thought by thinking how you think he might think. It's dizzying. If you haven't temporarily lost your mind, then you have seriously misplaced it. You are more lost and confused now than when you started this quest.

Darling, stop. His head is not a place for you to dwell. The truth of the matter is, he doesn't spend all that much time in there himself.

Men are different from women. It's why we love them and are fascinated by them. But (and we should all know this by now), they don't think like women think. We keep hoping that they do or that one day they will, but they don't. First of all, women can pretty much use both sides of the brain at the same time. Men have something like a three second delay. Men don't analyze their emotions the way women do. Unlike us, they don't walk around thinking about their feelings all day long — mainly because that would involve both the analytical and creative minds rapidly analyzing data. They just can't manage that as easily as women. It's like expecting them to put the seat *and* the lid down without being asked, or tell time *and* use the phone all on their own. It isn't going to happen naturally. But that's okay. Again, it's why we love them and are fascinated by them.

Yet, there you are in his brain, as a woman trying to think like a man, when a man rarely knows what he is thinking in the first place. Does that make any sense to you? Exactly. So, get out of his head. And, whatever you do, don't go back.

But What If...

But what if he told you he has a pattern of freaking out after six weeks/three months/two years? What if you know for sure he loves you and this is just a moment of panic?

Sweetie, that is not for you to decide or deal with. If he ended it, he needs to be the one to mend it. He doesn't need you, or well-meaning friends, to drop hints or help him along the road. If he doesn't have the stones to pick up the phone and make the apology, he's not the man for you.

But what if he does call and make the apology?

First of all, re-read The Ground Rules; you shouldn't be taking his calls for thirty days. There is a reason for that; it's to give you time to get your wits about you, friend. But, if in a moment of weakness you broke Rule #6, then tread wisely, kiddo. You don't want to be back in the same boat in another six weeks/three months/two years, do you?

Step 2
Don't Look for
Answers
Because There are
No Answers

Okay, you have successfully moved out of his head, but the *Why* and the *How* still haunt you. They follow you around like stray dogs looking for a home. They whine and paw and beg for attention...and they really need a bath. If only you could answer the *Why* or the *How*, then you would finally understand this tragedy and have some peace of mind.

You are a smart woman. You know that you can piece this puzzle together. Was it something you said? Did? Didn't do? Did you give too much? Not enough? Since you know better than to live in his head anymore, you've moved back into yours. After you've tidied up, you go over everything you did and said. Somewhere, there's an answer. And if you look hard enough or talk to the right people, you'll solve the riddle.

Every conversation you have with your friends, your family, your pet or yourself still contains a *Why* or a *How*.

Why didn't I see it coming?

How could I have been so wrong about him?

Why hasn't he called me?

How can he move on so easily?!?!

Perhaps you have noticed people are showing signs that they're losing patience with your inquisitive quest to answer the *Why* or the *How*. But you can't stop yourself. You are obsessed. There *has* to be a reason. You *need* to know the answers. If only you had the answers, then you could understand and get some closure.

Meticulously, you go over the breakup conversation(s) you had. Surely, you asked him *Why* or *How* at least once, right? You replay the questions and answers in your mind — or re-read them in the emails — but the answer he gave wasn't right. It was empty. Insincere. Unsatisfactory. He was protecting you. He was protecting himself. He wasn't being completely honest.

Then again, maybe he was. And what if he was? Does it really matter? More importantly, has any of this helped you feel better?

The fact is, there aren't any answers that will make you feel better about the end of your relationship. Try to imagine one. Did it work? What words could possibly make you feel better except for, "Please forgive me, I made a terrible mistake and I want you back"? And, if you'll notice, those words are not answers to either *Why* or *How.*

My friend, there are no answers. There just aren't. Logically, there should be but love is not logical. So, how could there be any answers?

Do yourself a service and stop searching for what's not there. You have better things to do with your life. Laundry even tops that fruitless effort. The sooner you stop, the faster you will get over him.

But What If...

What if you heard from a friend of yours, or his, that he explained why it ended and you think it's something you two can fix?

Well, men say a lot of things. Sometimes they say things just so they can hear the words come out of their mouths...especially if it puts them in a good light. Don't be fooled. If he wanted to, he would make the move to win you back and work it out. Again, he needs to do that on his own without "help" from you or friends.

If you really want to use your detective skills in this situation, why don't you take all that time and energy and solve the mystery of why you are still wasting so much time and energy on him?

Step 3
Don't Honor
Your Relationship
With Pain

Breakups hurt. There's no getting around that. They are sad, humiliating, disappointing and a downright bummer. All you can do is cry. You can't eat or sleep or function at work because the tears get in the way.

Breakups are not pretty. Your eyes are swollen. Your face is puffy. Makeup won't stay on; it just slides right off your skin. Your nose is red and chapped, and your upper lip appears to be donning a cherry-stained mustache that no amount of concealer will cover, even if it were able to stay on. You are a frightful sight. This is the one time in life that you are pretty much guaranteed to look as bad, if not worse, than you feel.

And you feel ghastly. You are in agony because you knew that this was *the* relationship. It was IT. He was the one and there isn't going to be another one like him. You are sure you will never feel that way about a man again. You will never know such a deep, fabulous, romantic, chemical, karmic connection...it was a once in a lifetime thing and now it's kaput! You find yourself deep in the heart of Never-Ever Land, certain that you will always be alone. Knitting afghans and mittens. Living with a dozen cats, or your endlessly irritating roommate.

Now, while you know all of the above is untrue, at times it feels that hopeless. You are mired in the suffering. You want the world to know that this relationship mattered. That it was important. It meant everything to you. In your greatest moments of doubt, you want to be reassured that it was real and that everything you heard and said and felt was true. The only way you can prove all that is by hurting and crying and wallowing in woe.

Stop. Right now. Just stop. Dry your eyes. Wipe your nose. Take a deep breath and collect yourself.

Let's dispel a lingering myth: The more

you hurt, the more valuable the relationship. It's a big fat lie. And it's a big fat lie that we allow ourselves and our friends to believe. How else can we rate a relationship except by how deeply we feel the pain when it ends?

The fact is, your relationship and your pain are not exponentially related. This kind of agony is not rational. It is not real. It is a vicious cycle perpetuated by phone calls to girlfriends while impaired on chocolate, Chianti and sadness.

Like it or not, time does heal. And just when you start feeling better, you think of something to make you feel worse, just to see if it does. It's like you are testing yourself to see if your heart is still broken. And if you cry, it is. A broken heart is not validation. It's victimizing.

Do not honor your relationship with tears and anguish, melancholy and misery. Take a moment to really understand what you are upset about. Broken hearts and battered egos feel an awful lot alike. And, as bad as it hurts, you are not mortally wounded. You are not bleeding. You can breathe. You will be fine. Stop with the waterworks and honor yourself with dignity. It causes less redness and swelling.

But What If...

What if the pain is more than you can handle? What if this is the worst pain you have ever felt? What if you can't shake it and grow more miserable each day?

Then you need to speak to a professional. No joke.

Sometimes a breakup can wake up past issues; stuff you thought was long ago healed. Don't hesitate to seek counselling. You shouldn't be suffering. You deserve better.

Step 4
Don't Pick the Scab

You are doing your best to stand strong. You've gone two whole days without crying (not counting the nights). But you miss him. You find yourself listening to the last message he left on voicemail. You re-read every email he sent. You look at the birthday cards. Read the love notes. Wear the jewelry. The lingerie. Order in from his favorite Thai place and drink the beer he left in your fridge. When you find his favorite movie playing on cable, you watch it even though you loathe it.

The collection of photos of the two of you in happy-couple poses has become a shrine. You listen to "our song" ad nauseam and create a playlist on your iPod of the music that served as the soundtrack to your time together. You rent sad, sappy DVDs and wash them down with Entenmann's. You might even drive by his house or his favorite bar, hoping to catch a glimpse of him...or at least his car. At the department store, you sneak a sniff of his cologne. At night, you sleep in the t-shirt he left behind. And all this does is make you even more miserable than the night it ended.

You are picking the scab, doll. Yes. As gross as it sounds, that's exactly what you are doing.

Think about what happens when you pick a scab. It bleeds. It might get infected. It won't heal properly. And when it finally does heal, after a long, long time, it leaves a scar, which sits as a reminder that you had gotten hurt but you didn't let yourself get better. You didn't trust nature to take her course. You didn't allow yourself to mend. And now you will have a skin-deep souvenir of that misstep and the mess you made of taking care of yourself.

Here's the best remedy to keep from picking that proverbial scab:

Take down his pictures immediately. Gather everything he ever gave you, every reminder of him, and put it all in a box in a dark corner of a closet that you can't easily get to. Turn off the light and shut the door. Forget that box is there. Delete his emails...ALL of his emails, including the replies you sent with his message included in the thread. Remove his number from speed dial and fill it with that of a good friend or Mr. MovieFone. If he left anything at your place, get a box or a bag and put it all in there; either give it to a friend to leave at his office, or mail it to him (no note). And that includes the t-shirt you've turned into a nightie.

This is an exorcism of sorts. It's not meant to be cold or spiteful, but protective of your broken heart. The fewer daily reminders you have of him and the "us" the two of you were, the better you will feel. And maybe in a few months' time, you can wear the dress he bought you without thinking of him when you do. But wait until you are really ready. Or have a really hot date to wear it on.

Of course you need to mourn the relationship. It is a loss. You are supposed to feel at least a sting if not an ache or a throbbing pain. You are entitled to a pity-party or two. But if you keep holding on to the pain, if you keep poking at the wound, it will keep bleeding. You don't want that. You don't want this healing to take any more time than absolutely necessary, do you? So listen to what your mother always said and quit picking at it!

But What If...

But what if you work together? Or live in a small town? The same building? What if all of your friends are his friends? What if you can't avoid reminders of him? How can you not pick the scab then?

If circumstances keep picking at you, maybe you need to make an escape. Take a vacation, even if it's merely a weekend at your aunt's house two towns away. Get away to get some distance from and perspective on the situation. A long weekend can work miracles — especially if spa treatments are involved. Never underestimate the power of a pedicure.

The key is not to have your focus on what hurts. Don't fixate on the relationship or him. Find something else to think about. Like you. A much more fascinating subject, don't you think?

You have to be stronger than the situation, my girl. And you are. Leave the hurt alone, and it will heal faster than you think.

Step 5
Accept the Truth

Clichés abound during a breakup. They persist because they hold some core truths. While the truth might hurt, it will also set you free. And nothing will make you feel better in this situation except for accepting the truth. Really. Once you accept it, you can get over it...and him.

There is one hard, universal truth of any breakup that few like to acknowledge, but one that is rather inescapable: *If the relationship was so great/perfect/wonderful, it would not have ended.*

Say it again, but now make it personal:

If our relationship was so great, it would not have ended.

Repeat as needed.

After the breakup, all you can think of is the good. You focus on the wonderful, the romantic, the loving and the sweet. But let's take a look at the annoying, the disappointing, the hurtful, the deceptive; these are the most important aspects to focus on. They are parts of the truth of your relationship, and its end.

The truth is, you knew it wasn't that great/perfect/wonderful. The truth is, there were problems. The truth is, there were challenges that would take two of you to overcome, and only one of you was doing the work (and that would probably be you). The truth is, some relationships were not built to last. The truth is, you have some responsibility here. Even if he was a total jerk, a cheat or an abuser, you have to take responsibility for not fully addressing the truth. And now you are doing it again.

The truth is, you weren't right for each other (and isn't it better to know that now rather than a year or two or five down the road?). The truth is, he let you down — not just when the relationship ended, but many times before that. The truth is, he wasn't completely honest with you. And, the truth is, you weren't completely honest with yourself. The truth is that all of this is okay. It's okay because, as prickly as it is, you are embracing the truth. Thank God! Hallelujah! Amen!

The truth is, you deserve better. The truth is, you wanted and needed more than he could give. The truth is, you didn't like his mother. The truth is, you thought his roommate was pretty hot. The truth is, as much as you had in common, you weren't all that compatible. The truth is, you had to compromise more than he did. The truth is, you had some really wonderful moments. The truth is, you had some really cruddy moments, too. And, the truth is, you are going to get over this and find a relationship that is truly wonderful for you.

But What If...

What if there were so many lies, you can't find the truth? Or what if the truth is so ugly you don't want to face it?

If you want, you can ignore the truth and stick your head in the sand like an ostrich, but do you know what happens then? Your derrière is left hanging out in the wind. You leave yourself vulnerable. And that's not a very attractive angle for anyone.

You have to find and face the truth. If it's too overwhelming for you to face alone, seek professional counsel. Really. The truth is important for so many reasons, but if the circumstance is traumatic (relating to abuse or past issues), don't go looking for it on your own if you aren't feeling strong. However, when you do find the truth and are able to accept it, you will feel like a new woman. A super woman!

One who can smell a lie on a guy at fifty paces and leap over a loser without a single rebound! And isn't that worth the introspection?

Step 6

Harness the Power of "So What?"

The two most powerful words in the English language are not "Abracadabra Shazaam". They are not "Open Sesame", or even "Pretty Please". The most magical, transformative words you can ever speak are: So what?

Say them aloud. So what. So what? SO WHAT! It's an empowering phrase, don't you think? Say it, sing it, feel it! *So futhermucking what?!?!* Don't you feel better? Go ahead, admit that you do. And so what! During the process of getting over him, make *So What* your personal mantra.

Your relationship ended horribly. So what?

You are alone and single again. So what?

He left you for someone else. So what?

He left you for no good reason. So what?

He left a message on your voicemail. So what?

He hasn't called or emailed you once. So what?

You've gained ten pounds. So what?

Your friends saw him out on a date. So what?

You bumped into his profile on an online dating site and he used a picture of the two of you and cropped you out! So what?

He is engaged, his fiancée is already pregnant, and it's only been three months since you broke up!!! Say it with me now...SO WHAT?

So what? So what about him, what he does or who he's with? So what?

The beautiful aspect of *So What* is that it deflates the meaning, the drama, the utter anxiety around an issue. So what if he's dating already? How does that truly affect your life (your life, not your ego)? It doesn't. Know why? Because he is no longer a part of your world. And so what? You deserve so much better.

So What comes in especially handy when an insensitive/instigating friend or bitchy coworker pokes a nose into your business. You know the ones; they want to keep you informed of his every move, their every theory and the latest statistics on single women and lightning strikes. Aren't they annoying? So, when someone serves you unpleasant information, just smile and say with a playful shrug, "So what?"

So What is a beautiful state of mind. When you say *So What*, it forces the heart, brain and ego into separate corners, and gives you a chance to think clearly for a change. You have to answer the question of "So what?" which naturally stymies the internal debate of how this breakup has ruined your life. Try to answer seriously a *So What* question. It's nearly impossible. And that should help you put it all into perspective. This really doesn't matter in the big picture of your life. It's just an unfortunate blip. And so what?

But What If...

What if *So What* didn't work and you are still hurting?

Then you need to have a good laugh, sister. Allow yourself to see the lighter side of things. Ask yourself if you aren't addicted to the drama and the attention that it brings.

Being a victim is easy. Standing tall after heartbreak takes strength and courage. And you know you are strong and courageous when you need to be. Like when you've worn those high heels on a night out before they were fully broken-in because you looked so damn good in them. Muster up that same bravery. If you can handle a half-dozen nickel-sized blisters, this breakup is a piece of cupcake.

Step 7
Know Your Worth

Now that your eyes are no longer swollen shut, you can take a good look at who you are. Go to the mirror and look yourself over. Take your time. Behold the beautiful and unique creature that you are. Observe all the characteristics you embody, all the talents and skills you possess. You are pretty damn incredible. And you are worth more than this pain. You are worth more than a relationship that was unhealthy, unsupportive, unfaithful, unrealistic, or even just un-fun.

Deep in the midst of your doldrums, you can easily forget who you are. How important you are. How magnificent, smashing and all around groovy, too. When you look at yourself now, you might not even recognize the person reflected back to you. You may wonder how the hell you got to such a state. Whatever you do, don't go down the road of blame. It doesn't matter the Who, the How, the Why and the What. All that matters right now is the You.

And you are amazing. You are special. You are truly one-of-a-kind. You are precious. And you know it. And you know that you deserve to be with a man who knows it, too.

Check the clock, pumpkin, because it's time for all the "poor me" poppycock to end. Seriously. If your friends haven't started to avoid your calls, they are on the verge of it. You are probably getting a little tired of the boo-hoo you, too.

You might still be hurting, but it's time to pull it together once and for all. The best way to do that is to remember to value you. While you might yet feel like gutter trash, you are far from that. So, take a long hot bath, go for a massage, get a facial or a manicure. Do something for you, something that reminds you that you are worth cherishing. You are someone to be treasured, worshipped and adored, and the most important person to do that is you. Not him. You.

You must know and believe in your heart of hearts that you are worth more than that pile of used tissues. More than the empty tubs of chunky caramel nutty ice cream piled in the bin. There are not enough chocolate covered candies in the universe to equate your worth, even if you go by calorie count. And don't you forget it. Really. It is time to end the endless pity-parties. Because you are worth grandly celebrating.

Okay, let's be honest. Perhaps some feelings of humiliation linger. It sucks to lose. And, without a doubt, you've had the whole of humanity giving you their two-cents on the matter. People react like you're a bird with a broken wing and tread lightly around you. They seem to have forgotten your name because you are only referred to as "poor girl". That just feeds into the bummer factor and you need to take a step back from that. You have to decide how you are going to define this, and whose opinion about you matters more: Yours or his? Yours or your mother's? Yours or your friends' and colleagues'? You need to take this time to center yourself and stand on your own two feet, firmly grounded in who you are.

You, my dear, are the one who sets your worth. And only you can mark it down. If you are moping around the house or can't drag your sorry self out of bed to make it to lunch with the girls, you are marking yourself down each day you behave that way. And while you are doing that to you, you are upping his value at the same time. Well, aren't you? Do you think he's crying in his beer? No. But you are one fudge-pop away from putting yourself in the emotional equivalent of a 99¢ sale box. Knock it off.

Not feeling me yet? Well, let's put it another way:

Say you spent your bonus on a beautiful pair of Manolo Blahnik 4-inch heeled, strappy sandals fit for a goddess (i.e., You). And let's say that one night out at a fabulous party, where you were having the time of your life, some buffoon walked by and spilled a bowl of bouillabaisse on those beautiful shoes. Luckily, your feet weren't scalded, but the shoes! Every inch of those fine stiletto heels were drenched in fish soup. What do you do? Wipe them off quickly so you can finish the night but then put them away in their box when you get home, stinking of the sea and saffron, never to see the light of day again because they are no longer perfect? Do you toss them out so you don't have to deal with the smelly, chunky mess? Or do you take the time to clean them properly, visit an expert if necessary, and give them a little extra TLC until they are back to their full splendor?

I would hope that you would rate yourself higher than a $700 pair of shoes.

Remember your worth. As a matter of fact, raise your worth. Because you have just survived an ugly part of love, and you are the better for it. You are worth more now than ever before. Be sure to honor that worth. Wallowing in self-pity is not honoring yourself. Seeking out pain is not honoring yourself. Eating too much, drinking too much, looking and feeling and behaving like *merde* is so not honoring your exquisite self. So, get over yourself. Go in and brush your hair (and maybe your teeth), put on a fabulous ensemble and call up a friend or five to go out with. You need to put yourself back in the spotlight.

But What If...

What if you are so mad at yourself for being so stupid for falling for his act that you think you deserve to feel lower than dirt? After all, it's your fault for being so blind.

Wrong. That is just the disco version of a pity-party.

While a breakup has a presence — one like a 300-pound gorilla — it is a past act. A second after it happens, it is history. It's your choice to marinate in the past. It's also your choice to wash the past from you and look forward to a fresh start.

It isn't always easy, but when you get knocked down, you have to muster your strength to get back up. This isn't any different from falling off a horse or eating cement from your Rollerblades. Dust yourself off, tend to your boo-boos and get back on your feet. You are worth at least that.

Step 8
Do Not Give Him Your Power

By now your sadness and pain might've melded into anger. You might begin craving justice more than *crème brulée*. By now you want him to know exactly how you feel and exactly what you think of him. And you are putting it all down on paper.

You have drafted the perfect letter, going over point-by-point every lie he told, every way he misled you, how much you gave to him, gave up for him and, as a matter of fact, he wasn't all that great in bed. You want him to know these things. It is your moral and civic duty to tell him so that no other woman suffers the same from him.

You've read and re-read and re-written the letter. It is as close to perfect as it is going to get. It's sitting on your desk in an envelope with his name on it. You just can't decide if you should mail it or leave it on his doorstep with a box full of the garbage he gave you, to fully illustrate your ire.

Well, before you send him that letter, you'd better get a bigger envelope so you can fit in your pride and dignity with it. Because mailing that letter is the equivalent of sending him your power. And that is the last thing you want to do.

Let's examine the intention behind the letter. What you want is not for him to know how you feel; you want to know how *he* feels. You want to know if he's feeling the same way. If he's sorry. If he thinks about you even half as often as you think about him.

What you expect is for him to read that letter and understand how badly he hurt you, and to feel bad about it. But that won't happen. Why? Because you are expecting him to react like a woman. To over-think things like a woman. You know that if you got a letter like the one you've written him, you would pick up the phone, tell him how awful you were feeling about the whole thing, and that you'd like to get together and talk. But that's because you are a woman. And, unless you've picked up the wrong book, your ex doesn't have a uterus.

Giving a man "the letter" is giving him the upper hand. Sadly, you will not get the reaction you are hoping for. And it will not make you feel better. At the end of the day, you will most likely feel worse. In a moment of clarity, which usually happens once you drop the letter into a postbox or press *Send*, you will realize that what you did was not powerful, it was pathetic...and quite possibly humiliating, depending on how detailed the letter was. If you want to show a man how little he matters to you or how over him you are, a letter is the worst way to do it.

Sometimes the urge to rant and get it all out is overwhelming, so if you need to write a letter, write a letter **but**...save it for a day or two, and then read it again with fresher eyes. How does it sound now? Glad you didn't send it? I thought so. And now that you are done with it, barbecue it. If you need to, write another letter, and another and another...do it until you get all that nasty resentment out. But never ever ever ever under any circumstances send him one. Burn, shred, delete or otherwise destroy every draft of every letter. Trust me, even you won't want to read those in the future.

As much as you might wish it would, the letter won't deliver him a lesson. It will simply give him an ego stroke. And do you really want to do that? Of course not. Keep it in your mind that he doesn't deserve your thoughts or your energy anymore. Even if you want to say something nice, don't. It's over, darling. And you are on your way to getting over it.

But What If...

What if you already sent him the letter or made the late-night-three-Apple-Martini phone call?

Whoopsie.

Okay, so you had a lapse in judgment. It happens. Just don't let it happen again.

Perhaps the letter or call you made was saturated in venom, and you feel you need to do a little damage control. If you sounded crazy or said some truly horrible things, maybe you should send a brief — and I do mean short, sweet and to the point — email saying, "I apologize. I didn't mean what I said." And that's it. Anything more would be another lapse in judgment that your integrity may not survive.

If damage control isn't required, and all you are feeling is a bit of embarrassment and remorse, let sleeping dogs lie. He probably blew it off, and so should you.

No matter what, don't let this become a back-and-forth line of angry and/or weepy communication between the two of you. That will get you nowhere. If he contacts you regarding the letter, reply with the simple apology mentioned above. If he persists, don't engage. Ignore it. Block him from your email or change your number.

Step 9
Learn the Lesson, Lose the Rest

Of course it wasn't all bad. There were good times in that relationship. You two shared some very special moments. He could be absolutely wonderful...when he wasn't being an absolute ass. You don't need to forget the good. Just don't dwell on it. You don't even need to hate him. Just take him down from that pedestal and remove the shining armor while you're at it.

You got together for a reason, and it ended for a reason. It may be hard to name the reason, but, if you give it a bit of a think, chances are you already know what it is. It was that little thing nagging at you for some time now. The pebble in your shoe that you couldn't shake away. And while there are no answers, there is always a lesson. You just need to uncover it.

This may be like sorting through a sale rack to find your size, but the lesson is in there somewhere. Learning it will set you firmly on your feet and you will never have to relive this particularly awful experience ever again.

Maybe the lesson is listening to your gut. We women can become confused by the conflicting information sent from our heads and our hearts. One or the other can mislead us, but our gut will never let us down. It's like Yoda lives in our solar plexus. When there is a pesky sensation in the pit of your stomach, believe it. (It has yet to lead me wrong.)

Perhaps this was a repeat offense. Maybe you caught him in a lie early on and chose to let it go out of love. Then you started lying to yourself to cover for him when more lies came. Or maybe, in spite of the warning signs and similarities to the last three guys you dated, you stayed with him because you were determined to make this relationship work. Honey, that's like trying to milk a bull. Not only is it futile, it's bound to get you hurt.

My friend, learning the lesson isn't about blaming yourself or even him; it's about

68

understanding. And that is empowerment. Once you learn the lesson, hallelujah, you can let go of all the rest. All the sadness and anger and resentment merely weighs you down, and the only person hurting from it is *you*. That negative energy isn't making it all the way across town to him. It's rotting inside you, like that forgotten doggie bag in the back of your refrigerator, causing a wicked stench. Blech. Let me tell you, other men can smell that. Yes, they can. Ask them. They can smell wounded and bitter a mile away.

Unfortunately, you can't un-ring a bell. With all of our technical advances, they still haven't invented a time machine that will let you go back to the past and change things. And, as much as you would like to hear him say it, "sorry" doesn't fix a damn thing. So, grab on to the lesson and release everything else.

Letting go isn't that hard. It's the anxiety leading up to the letting go that's tough. It's similar to how bad you feel right before you barf. Such a wretched feeling. But then, with a cramp and a lurch, you do it. You let it all go. It can be quick or it can seem endless. Yet, after it's over, you feel better than you thought you would or could. You are overcome with a sense of lightness and relief because you are no longer bloated with all that rancid poison. And though you are reluctant to admit it, it was worth how bad you felt in order to feel that good again.

Letting go only feels scary if you've made the pain a security blanket. There's a comfort in what you know; and if you know hurt and disappointment too well, it's easy to stay with them. Why move on at all? The sofa is comfy and the pizza guy throws in free garlic cheese bread every now and then. Maybe, now that you think about it, this isn't so bad after all? At least you won't have to worry about getting hurt again.

Please.

At some point you have to dump all the past crap you've been dragging around like the rubbish it is. It's too much of a hassle to haul it around, anyway. Even airlines charge you for bringing on too much baggage. Your personal B.S. should have a weight limit, too.

The lesson is the only souvenir you should keep. It is the most precious thing given to you from that relationship. The lesson will serve as your foolproof vest, keeping the same kind of joker from coming into your life. With it, you will be able to better protect yourself from making those less-than-fabulous choices in the men you date. And wouldn't you pay full price for that?

But What If...

What if there isn't a lesson to be found? What if this relationship was just a complete waste of time?

Sorry to hear that. I detest wasting time, so I can imagine your irritation. But are you sure it's not the anger talking here? You really can't take anything positive away from this relationship? Even if it's something as simple as that you learned not to take rejection like this personally?

Okay, if you are absolutely certain that there is not a single lesson to be found here, then put it all behind you, girlfriend. Congratulations! You are so over him.

But, if that's true, then why are you still crying?

You are almost there. You are getting over him.

Just one more step to go...

Step 10
Move On

Now that you are out of his head, you've stopped looking for answers that don't exist, and you aren't wallowing in agony or picking scabs; now that you've embraced the truth and know that *So What* has magical powers; now that you value your worth, have kept your power and learned the lesson, there is nothing left for you to do but move on.

A new chapter has begun, my dear. There's nothing but opportunity on the road ahead. This isn't just fluffy talk, it's true.

Believe it or not, we have a say in how we live and what happens to us. We really do. No matter what comes your way, you can choose to be miserable or be totally blissed out. Sure, life will throw an obstacle at you every now and then — just to keep you on your toes — but it's up to you how to handle it. It's your choice to let that obstacle stop you in your tracks or to use it as a stepladder to move up and on to something greater.

Everything is possible now, including finding a great guy. If you want to find love, open yourself up to it. Don't make a list of likes and dislikes or paint a picture in your head of what Mr. You looks like. That's how you got into trouble in the first place. Let it happen without grand expectation. Relax. Dating should be much simpler than we make it out to be. If you want a relationship with a wonderful man, don't accept a relationship with a man who is not wonderful. And toss out every fairytale you've ever read. Nothing has ruined women more than the "happily ever after" fantasy we've been fed since we were toddlers. So, when you are moving on, leave Snow White, Cinderella, Sleeping Beauty and Prince Charming behind. What you want is real. And real doesn't always come in a picture-perfect package.

By the way, in case you haven't copped on to this yet, "happily ever after" takes a hell of lot of work. Don't check out once you get into a relationship. Stay present. Address problems. Confront issues. Never forget who you are, what you are worth and to always honor yourself...as well as each other. (And don't be afraid to get professional help when needed. You take your car to a mechanic when it's not running right, don't you? Exactly. Enough said.) Take your time before diving back into a relationship, though. You wouldn't want to rebound yourself right back into another heartbreak. Pace yourself. And have a good time while you are at it.

So, how exactly do you move on? Well, that depends on you. Some gals take classes in a subject or language they've always wanted to learn. Some take on a new hobby or skill. Others throw themselves into work or go on a fabulous vacation. But all it really takes is a few good friends and a Saturday night or three out, *et voila!* You have moved on. It doesn't take much more than wanting to move on to actually do it.

Warning: A debate may begin between your common sense and your emotional state when you first start moving on. Your heart and your head might go into battle. If that happens and you find yourself on shaky ground, picture your physical totem pole. Your head is the top dog. It trumps your heart. At times like these, it should. And though your vagina may chime in on the matter, don't listen to her. Not only is she low-man on the totem pole, she has been known to make some terrible decisions... especially after last call.

Your happiness is a decision. It's not a twist of fate, nor is it held in the hands of a man. It's all on you, baby. It's your life. Live it like you mean it.

But What If...

What if you just can't move on? What if he is all that you ever wanted and now the dream you had of a fabulous future is gone...and your hope of ever knowing happiness again went with it?

That sounds pretty melodramatic, don't you think?

Let's talk about real loss. Death is a real loss. Have you ever lost a family member or a dear friend suddenly? That is a devastating experience. Breakups can feel similar, especially when it happens without warning. It is a loss, but the difference is both of you are still alive, drawing breath and greeting new days. Your life hasn't ended; your relationship has. Get this into perspective. Stop making this bigger than it is.

There is happiness and pleasure to be found. If you choose to stay mired in the cesspool of the breakup, fine. It's a free country. But be prepared to lose much more than your boyfriend. You are risking your self-respect, your self-esteem, friendships and your future bliss. Are you really willing to risk losing all that over the guy who was dumb enough to have dumped you? Please. Go back to Page 1 and start all over again. I'm not giving up on you yet.

In Closing...

If you found some of the sections to be glib, I apologize. But after a breakup, sometimes what you need is salt, not sugar. You need to gain a clear perspective on the situation. Friends are doing the best they can to support you, but what would help you most is a reality check you can cash.

You be might thinking, "Ha, what does this broad know about breakups?" Or you may believe that I have ice water pumping through my veins and, thus, no clue about how bad you really feel. Oh, but I do. I chose not to pepper the book with my stories or the tales of other broken-hearted women because, like I said in the beginning, this book is about you. However, just to give you some proof that I do feel your pain, let me tell you my favorite breakup line, which was delivered by a man that I had known for several years and whom I dated — in an off-on manner — for a year-and-a-half.

"Dick" and I sat on my sofa. We were having a long and rational conversation about what we both wanted out of a relationship, and where this one was headed, when he looked me in the eye and said, "You know, you are everything I have ever wanted in a woman, but I don't want you."

Oof. Now those are some strong words and they hit me like a fist. Fortunately, my first thought was not, "Oh my God, what did I do wrong?" or "Good grief, how can I fix this?" My first thought was, "Wow, what a...Dick."

I think Dick expected me to tear up, or at least blow up, but I actually smiled and said, "Well, Dick, if that's how you feel, there's the door. Don't knock on it again." Dick sat there a bit confused and didn't move until I told him I was serious. I got up, opened the door and waited for him to exit through it. And as soon as I closed it behind him, sans the melodramatic slam, I collapsed on the sofa in tears. What an awful way to be dumped! A pseudo compliment followed by a swift kick in the ego. Only a complete Dick could say something so cruel. And that meant I had loved a complete Dick. Tragically, I really thought this Dick was The One. We had a history. A long and unrelenting attraction to each other. It seemed fated. I had never known such happiness, passion and intensity, nor had I been with a man with whom I felt so comfortable. I could be my full self with him...how novel! I whole-heartedly believed that we would be able to work it out (since we had so much in common and wanted the same things out of life and had such a good time when we weren't fighting) and (once he worked out his career problems) that it would lead to something he and I both wanted, and what friends had long-predicted: Marriage.

That abysmal breakup helped me understand what was my responsibility and what was his personal mound of manure. I broke a pattern with him, and I am grateful for what I learned. That pathetic ending was a true beginning for me. Yet it was a dumping that I did which served me an even greater lesson.

I met "Romeo" online — a venue I have very little faith in. I had set out to prove my friend wrong about it, but ended up finding a great guy. He was everything I had ever wanted in a man and more. Except he was divorced. And I was the first woman he was intimate with after the divorce, which had occurred a year earlier. When I cried, "Rebound!" he assured me this was indeed what he wanted and was ready for. I listened to him rather than my gut. Mistake.

We fell hard and fast. It was organic, nothing forced. Never once did I have to take its temperature or ask, "Where is this going?" There was no need. It was unfolding naturally, beautifully, just as I believed it should. Then, one night, giddy as a schoolgirl, I signed on to the site to send my friend in France a link so she could see how cute he was. Not only was Romeo "Online Now!", he had added new photos to his profile. And this was after we had agreed to be monogamous and had our blood tests!

Since he was online, I emailed him immediately. The subject line simply read, "Disappointed". I outted myself for my seventh-grade antics and explained how I was saddened by his actions. To be honest, I knew why he did it. It was an ego stroke. And when we talked a few moments later, he admitted he wanted to see how many women were checking him out, and that was all it was. While he did his best to explain and apologize, the trust I had for him was broken. I didn't believe he was ready for a committed relationship. And I wasn't sure I would be able to trust him again. So I ended it. I hung up the phone, went over to his house, picked up my stuff and left him his. I wouldn't let him hug me, and I wouldn't let myself cry. I figured if I pulled the plug, I wasn't in a position to do the boo-hoo.

I made it a week before I let the tears flow like mini rivers. By then I had done a lot of thinking. I knew I wasn't crying just for the end of that relationship, but for the disappointment of all the broken hearts that came before. I was crying for me, not him. And that understanding was a great relief.

Getting over a breakup is hard but not impossible. And it doesn't have to take weeks or months or years to get over it either. Take it step-by-step, and, before you know it, you are over it.

The wisest, most self-preserving thing you can do is to give up on finding closure. Closure, when it comes to the end of a relationship, is like a unicorn — a very nice myth that I have yet to see. Peace of mind, however, is achievable, but only if you allow yourself to have it. Time and patience are your best allies. Each day it gets better if you let it. Just have faith. What is waiting for you is better than your wildest dreams. Better because it will be real.

I have one last caveat for you: Do NOT agree to be friends with him. There is no need to be involved in something that is potentially hurtful. You weren't friends before, so why be friends after? Even if you were friends before, you have plenty of friends. You don't need him creeping about. Friendship with an ex isn't possible without a long passage of time. This isn't to say you need to dislike him or be his enemy, but you need to see that type of "friendship" as anything but.

Men generally want to "be friends" after a breakup for two reasons:

1. To be sure you don't think he's a jackass (men never like to be thought of that way, the ego can't stand it); and

2. They want to keep tabs on you or, in some

cases, keep you on a leash (anytime you move on a bit, they try to reel you back in).

Don't fall for the "friendship" fraud. You need to break all contact for a while (re-read *The Ground Rules*) to allow yourself to heal, get a clear perspective and regain your emotional strength. Otherwise you risk ending up in bed with him, thinking that roll in the hay was a get-back-together celebratory romp, when it was really just a familiar shag. And that's worse than sending the letter.

Speaking of the letter, why don't you write one to yourself? In it make a list of your ten core values. Then make a list of ten goals you would like to accomplish in your lifetime. Stick these lists on your refrigerator or somewhere you can glance at them daily, and be sure the next man you get serious about fits in with those two Top 10s. The man you really want, the one who will bring you the most joy, is the man who respects your beliefs and will support you enthusiastically in achieving your dreams. And that's way better than some guy in tights kissing you out of a coma or returning your lost shoe.

You, my friend, are going to be fine. But if you are sitting on the sofa watching reality T.V. marathons, you might miss finding your bliss. Get off your butt! Get out there and revel in the fact that you have gotten over him! Go on. Crack open the champagne, do a happy dance and embrace all that awaits you. The future's as bright and beautiful as you are.

I wish you the very best.

Biographies...

About the Author

A Los Angeles native and graduate of the California Institute of the Arts, Sandra Ann Miller toiled in the film industry prior to her writing career...and the stories she could tell if not for the confidentiality agreements. After a decade in Hollywood, working on everything from *Pumpkinhead II* to *Alien Resurrection*, and for actors, managers and company chiefs, she began working as a freelance copywriter and consultant for individuals, non-profits and small businesses.

In addition to *A Sassy Little Guide to Getting Over Him*, Sandra writes for her long-running website, www.RUAWAKE.com, and is in the process of completing her first novel, *Chainsmoking Vegetarians & Other Annoyances in L.A.* A real, live, Internet-ordained minister, she remains the go-to gal when friends are tied up in a breakup crisis or are tying the knot.

Sandra lives and enjoys bouts of serial monogamy in Venice, California. You can reach her through MySpace at:

www.MySpace.com/MsWriteNow

www.MySpace.com/GetOverHim

About the Artist

Michiko Stehrenberger specializes in creating character designs for fashion and entertainment clients such as MTV, Sony Pictures, Burton Snowboards, PlayStation, Ford's *Race for the Cure*, and Tokyo's Yellow Boots clothing line. After earning her BFA in Illustration with honors from the Art Center College of Design in Pasadena, and spending over a decade drawing for her supper in New York City, she is now happily giving it up to learn the art of Honda repair in the boondocks of Washington State.

Her trademark series of BimBionic characters – 'Perfect Girls for an Imperfect World' – have appeared nationwide on MaxRacks circulated free postcards since 1995. Design and licensing inquiries regarding "Boots" (cover art) and other characters are thoroughly welcomed at:

www.michiko.com